BASIC

POWER POINT

STEP BY STEP GUAID LINES TO UNDERSTAND POWER POINT

DEDICATION

I DEDICATED THIS

BOOK TO ALL MY

READERS

ACKNOWLEGEMENT

All praise and adoration is due to nobody except almighty God

the lord of mankind. I praise him and glorified him for is

protections and blessings over me so far. And also for giving me

opportunities to create this small work, for the benefit of my

readers. I am also indebted to my late father for his

tremendous efforts to make my education successful. May his

gentle soul continue to rest in perfect peace till eternity

(amen). And also to my great mother for her intensive supports

on very steps I take. May she live long to eat the fruit of her labor. This work would not have seen the light of the day if not

for the prayers, patronage and encouragement of my readers. I

thank you all, may almighty god in his infinity mercy continue

and protect every one of us (amen).

What is PowerPoint?

Microsoft PowerPoint is without a doubt the most famous

application used to give introductions. You're probably going to

see PowerPoint introductions utilized for everything from the

world's biggest organizations to grade teachers sharing

examples.

PowerPoint is much of the time the victim of the joke. Many

discredit PowerPoint as exhausting and a support for

ineffectively pre-arranged speakers.

Just a terrible craftsman faults the instruments. Furthermore,

similar to any instrument, PowerPoint is staggeringly valuable

when utilized appropriately. You can involve it as a guide on

your talking commitment to construct solace and drive focuses

outwardly with your crowd.

Show

A good to go moderator can utilize PowerPoint to fabricate

outlines and charts, for instance.

In this instructional exercise, we will zero in on working within

PowerPoint to construct a show. To dominate the application,

we'll discuss and cover the most well-known stages a

tenderfoot PowerPoint client has to be aware.

Here are the key moves you'll have to make to construct a

PowerPoint show:

You'll have to add slides, the singular pages in the show.

You'll add content to the slides, for example, text boxes,

pictures, outlines and charts.

Change subjects and styles to make your show look proficient

and fit the event in question.

Plan show helps like Speaker Notes and Moderator View to

assist you with feeling OK with introducing.

We'll cover every one of these in this PowerPoint instructional

exercise so you can make ready rapidly.

Promotion

Step by step instructions to Explore PowerPoint

To find a workable pace with PowerPoint, it assists with

understanding the design of the application. We should stroll

through the key menu choices with the goal that you can learn

PowerPoint rapidly. Assuming you comprehend the way that

the application is spread out, you're probably going to find any

component you really want rapidly.

We should investigate the vital pieces of PowerPoint's point of

interaction.

1. The Lace

The lace menu is seen as across a considerable lot of

Microsoft's applications, like Word, Succeed, and PowerPoint. It

lives over the primary region of the application.

PowerPoint Strip screen capture model

The PowerPoint strip allows you to switch between different

tabs.

The strip holds back a progression of tabs that you can switch

between. Each of these have an interesting arrangement of

devices to distinctively work with your show. At the point when

you switch tabs on the lace, you'll see new fastens and choices

to adjust your show:

Document - save, offer, and product your show.

Home - a universally useful assortment of the most widely

recognized devices that you'll use in PowerPoint.

Embed - an across the board device to add each envision

capable kind of satisfied, like tables, pictures, graphs, video,

and that's just the beginning.

Plan - controls the general look and feel of your show with topic

and style settings.

Advances - add activitys when you switch slides.

Movements - controls the request and style that articles will

enter or leave your slide with.

Slide Show - control settings connected with the manner in

which your show seems while imparting it to a crowd of people.

Now that you comprehend the format, you have a superior

thought of how you can leap to the element you want. We

should jump a piece further into how you can utilize a few of

these key tabs.

2. The Home Tab

Use it for: an overall determination of the most famous devices

in PowerPoint.

I typically stay on the Home tab while I'm working in

PowerPoint. The explanation is on the grounds that it has

essentially every device you really want. From adding another

slide to changing text and passage settings, the Home tab is the

default for most clients.

Home on Lace

The Home tab has large numbers of the most generally utilized

devices, across the board bar.

3. The Supplement Tab

While you're dealing with adding content to a slide, the

Supplement tab has each conceivable device to add new happy

to a slide. Pick one of these kinds of objects to add it to the

slide.

Embed tab PowerPoint strip

The Supplement tab has the instruments you want to add

tables, pictures, outlines, and that's just the beginning.

4. Sees

PowerPoint has various perspectives which are essentially

various ways of working with a similar show. You can change

the view to get an alternate point of view on your substance.

Use sees for an alternate method for editting and fabricate

your PowerPoint show.

Sees tab

The Perspectives tab really impacts the viewpoint on your

PowerPoint show.

In the screen capture underneath, you can see the contrast

between the default Ordinary view and Slide Sorter view.

Ordinary view shows each slide up front, while slide sorter view

makes thumbnails that you can move to reorder the show.

Ordinary and Slide Sorter sees

Typical view is the default show view in PowerPoint, while an

other view like Slide Sorter permits you to re-succession your

show by moving the slide thumbnails.

5. The Plan Tab

An alluring show can truly catch your crowd's eye. We use

subjects and styles in PowerPoint to add visual enticement for

the show, and the Plan tab truly controls these settings.

Plan Tab PowerPoint

Click on one of the subject thumbnails to change the look and

feel of the show.

On the Plan tab, you can tap on one of the subjects to restyle

the show. Or on the other hand, evaluate an alternate Style

thumbnail to upgrade the variety subject.

The Moves toward Building a PowerPoint

We've handled the point of interaction of PowerPoint, so you

ought to feel quite alright with how to get around the

application. Presently, we should discuss the activities you'll

wind up utilizing more than once and how you can do that in

PowerPoint.

1. Instructions to Add Slides

Consider slides the singular units in your show that you can

load up with content. To embed another slide, go to the

Addition tab on PowerPoint's lace. Then, at that point, click on

the New Slide button to add another slide to your show.

New Slide Added

Another slide will have essential placeholders to add your

substance to in PowerPoint.

Every one of the thumbnails that you'll see on the sidebar

addresses a slide. Then, at that point, you'll add content to each

slide.

There's no pragmatic breaking point to the quantity of slides

that your PowerPoint document can contain. Nonetheless, you

ought to consider the number of slides it that really takes to

come to your meaningful conclusion. It's frequently the

2. Step by step instructions to Add Content

Content characterizes every single slide. PowerPoint obliges an

extensive variety of content like text, diagrams, tables, graphs,

and then some.

The most straightforward method for adding content is to get

going by picking a Design, which you can browse the Home tab.

PowerPoint designs

Different PowerPoint designs displayed on the Home tab.

These designs have content boxes that are not difficult to add

your own substance to. Basically pick a design, and afterward

begin adding your substance.

3. Instructions to Pick a Subject and Style

After you work out your show's substance, it's smart to

contemplate adding visual style. For this, you'll get around to

the Plan tab, and snap on one of the thumbnails for a subject.

PowerPoint topic dropdown

Utilize the Plan tab to pick a subject.

Utilizing a PowerPoint subject is the favored option in contrast

to adding foundations, variety and type styles to every single

slide. Changing the topic regularly will change the whole show

at the same time. This incredibly lessens the time engaged with

building a show.

With simply these three stages, you have the repeatable

succession of activities expected to fabricate a show.

Instructions to Enhancer PowerPoint

With each inventive application I've at any point realized, there

are dependably those insider subtle strategies that you learn

numerous months after the fact. They spread the word about

you wish that you had them from the start and ponder the

numerous hours you squandered on the expectation to learn

and adapt.

PowerPoint is no special case for this standard, and you

genuinely must can get straight to the point while you're

hurrying to plan for your show.

The most effective way to save time on your show is to begin

with a pre-constructed PowerPoint subject. Furthermore, you

can find those on Envato Components, which is a limitless

download administration for creatives.

PowerPoint Introductions Rundown on Components

Envato Components incorporates north of 700 PowerPoint

topics as a feature of everything you-can-download level rate

administration.

Presently, the majority of the records that you'll get from the

Components PPTX subjects will have all the earmarks of being

done introductions. You may be considering how to involve

these pre-assembled introductions for your own requirements.

To utilize Components subjects, it's actually about chopping it

down to the slide plans that you'll utilize. A superior topic is truly about the thoughts that are incorporated as a feature of

it. Basically utilize these thoughts as beginning stages that you

can add your own substance to.

Volt Components Model

The Volt PowerPoint topic is one of more than 700 included as

a component of an Envato Components membership, and

elements 120 slide plans you can use for yourself.

Once more, the worth of Components is that you can download

however many documents as you need while you're an

endorser. What's more, assuming that you quit buying in, you'll

in any case reserve the option to utilize the imaginative

resources you got. It's a lot quicker than building each slide

without any preparation.

Apparatuses for Moderators

The substance and configuration will differ enormously from

one show straightaway. In any case, regardless of what the

objective of your show is, there are normal devices that each

moderator can profit from utilizing.

How about we center around the most significant apparatuses

for speakers in this PowerPoint instructional exercise. I

generally notice these devices as a method for building

certainty and solace for moderators.

1. Speaker Notes

Disregard working out note cards or keeping a printed frame

close by. Speaker notes are a method for adding the things you

want to say to each slide.

Speaker notes are added to every individual slide, and the most

ideal way to add them is from Ordinary view. Click on Notes

beneath the show region and type your slide-explicit notes.

MICROSOFT POWERPOINT

The most effective method to Add Speaker Notes to

PowerPoint in 60 Seconds

Andrew Childress

Speaker notes will appear in printed duplicates of your show, so

it's more straightforward to incorporate them into PowerPoint

as opposed to writing note cards you might lose.

2. Moderator View

Another element that is a must-utilize is Moderator View,

which is ideal for two screen arrangements while introducing.

While your crowd will see the show you've based on the

projector or LCD screen, you'll have your own confidential view

with speaker notes, forthcoming slides and that's just the

beginning.

Divert on Moderator View from the slideshow tab by clicking

Use Moderator View.

Illustration of PowerPoint Moderator View

An illustration of PowerPoint Moderator View.

Look at a full aide underneath on maximizing Moderator View:

MICROSOFT POWERPOINT

Instructions to Give a PowerPoint Slideshow Moderator View

Andrew Childress

3. Spelling and Punctuation Check

There's nothing more regrettable than missing a vital mistake

before you give your show. To keep away from this issue, it's an

extraordinary assistance to run a spelling and punctuation

check before you give your show.

To check for normal spelling issues, basically leap to the Audit

tab and snap Spelling. PowerPoint will check for the most

widely recognized issues and permit you to address them on a

case by case basis.

MICROSOFT POWERPOINT

The most effective method to Spell-Check Your PowerPoint

Slides in 60 Seconds

Andrew Childress

Recap and Continue To learn

This PowerPoint instructional exercise assisted you with making

headway with utilizing Microsoft PowerPoint, with the means

for making slides and the easy route to a superior show with

pre-constructed subjects.

At Tuts+, we've been working out a progression of PowerPoint

instructional exercises that can assist you with building your

show abilities. On the off chance that you're having an

apprehensive outlook on giving a show for your work or

independent practice, evaluate a greater amount of these

instructional exercises like the ones underneath.